Your Biggest Questions About Pok mon Go Plus Answered!

Pok mon Go Plus is a device that lets Pok mon Go players perform some in-game actions without pulling out their phones. After being paired with a phone, it will vibrate when you're near a pok stop and let you collect items from it, and it will flash when a pok mon is near, after which you can press a button to throw a pok ball. So how much will it cost, where can you get one, what can you do with it and how can you get the best use out of your Pok mon Plus? In this guide, we everything you need to know and all your burning questions about Pok mon Go and the Plus Accessory answered!

Table of Contents

What is the Pokémon Go Plus? ... 3
So what exactly does it do? ... 3
So You Say the Plus Can help me catch Pokémon? ... 3
Do I need Pokemon Go Plus? ... 4
Will Pokemon Go Plus work with my phone? ... 5
What are the Pokemon Go Plus' specifications? ... 5
What should I do in the meantime? ... 5
What the heck is Pokémon Go? ... 6
So how do I get started? ... 6
What Pokémon Creatures Will I Encounter? ... 8
How do I catch my first Pokémon? ... 8
Isn't walking around with my eyes glued to my phone dangerous? ... 9
How do I capture a Pokémon? ... 10
What are Pokémon 'items' and how do I use them? ... 11
How do I check-in at pokestops? ... 12
How easy is the game on my phone battery? ... 12
How do I know which Pokémon is available to me? ... 13
How do I Track a Pokémon? ... 14
How do I use Pokéstops? ... 16
What Pokémon Go Doesn't tell you. ... 18
How do I level up and evolve my Pokémon? ... 21
How do I join a Gym team and battle other players? ... 22
How do I level up as a trainer? ... 23
Do you need the Pokémon Go Plus wearable? ... 24
Troubleshooting Pokémon Go ... 24
How to fix Pokémon Go crashes ... 25
   Try to leave the app and come back ... 27
   Reboot and bug report ... 29
How to stop Pokémon Go from draining your battery ... 29
   Turn on the Battery Saver option ... 30
   Turn off Augmented Reality ... 32
   Get a battery case ... 32
How do I play Pokémon Go when I get a server error ... 32
In conclusion ... 33

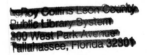

What Pokémon Go Plus?

Pokémon GO Plus is a small device that lets you enjoy Pokémon GO while you're on the move and not looking at your smartphone. The Pokémon Go Plus is priced at $34.99 at launch resembles a Pokéball mixed with a Google Maps pin, which is a brilliant motif of the game's combination of Pokémon and real world travel. It uses Bluetooth to connect to your smart device, and you can clip it to your lapel or wear like a bracelet to stay connected to your game at all times. The Plus notifies you about events in the game—such as the appearance of a Pokémon nearby—using an LED and vibration. You can think of it as a Pokémon flavored smart watch. It can even be used to catch the Pokémon itself so you don't even have to take your phone out of your pocket.

So What Exactly Does It Do?

The Plus lets you know when you're near a PokeStop (the specially marked locations on the game's map that come with items, Pokémon eggs and, if you're lucky, Pokémon to catch). When a Pokémon is near, the light on the Pokémon GO Plus will flash. It will also flash and vibrate when you pass a Poke Stop. Once a Pokémon is close, press the button on the Pokémon GO Plus to throw a Pokéball. You'll only be able to throw a Pokéball using Pokémon GO Plus if you've caught the Pokémon before. The Pokémon GO Plus will flash and vibrate to let you know if you were successful in catching the Pokémon

So You Say The Plus Can Help Me Catch Pokémon?

In a way, yes! The Pokémon Go Plus allows you to catch Pokémon without taking out your phone. If a Pokémon is nearby, the device will light up. At that point, you can throw a Pokéball, just by using the device. This only works if you've already caught that Pokémon before, though; you won't be catching any new Pokémon for your Pokédex using the Pokémon Go Plus. If it worked out, the Plus will vibrate to celebrate your achievement.

Do I Need Pokemon Go Plus?

Because it is an extension of Pokémon Go, you don't need the Plus to get the whole experience - you simply need a smartphone for the game itself. Instead, it can help make the search for PokeStops and Pokémon easier and more comfortable. If you wear one on your wrist, for example, you can go about your daily life, occasionally stopping whenever it tells you a Pokémon is nearby.

So when does the Pok mon Go Plus come out? And how can I get one?

The manufacturers have not given an official release date yet but they have said it will be sometime in September 2016. Nintendo's GameStop website is the only confirmed retailer for the Plus right now, and the $34.99 device recently went up for pre-order there, where it was listed for a July 31 release. Toward the end of July, however, Nintendo of America tweeted that the peripheral wouldn't hit stores until September 2016.

Although the July release had long been teased, September is the first explicit confirmation of a release window from the publisher. It sold out quickly. It's currently unavailable on Amazon but you can set a notification on Amazon so that you get an email the moment it's available. Resellers are offering the Plus for more than three times the retail price on eBay but since the device has not been released yet, we can assure you that these people don't have it to sell. So be careful about buying it on ebay (or anywhere else) because you might fall prey to scammers. We will suggest you wait until it is officially released before purchasing it via these mediums. You'll definitely be paying too much if you buy it anywhere above the official $34.99 price.

Will Pokemon Go Plus Work With My Phone?

On launch, Pok mon Go Plus will work with both Android and iPhones. Basically, if your phone can download the game, the Plus will work with it.

What Are The Pokemon Go Plus' Specifications?

Inside the pack you get the Pokemon Go Plus device, a polyester wristband that measures 4-7cm when worn, and a removable CR2032 Lithium coin cell battery for power. The device itself, which looks like the pointer in the app, is 46 x 33 x 17.5mm and weighs 13g.

What Should I Do In The Meantime?

You can keep playing Pok mon Go! You can still enjoy the game even if you don't have the Plus yet. If you are new to Pok mon Go revolution, check out our tips and tricks of how you can get the best out of the game in the pages that follow.

What the heck is Pok mon Go?

Pok mon GO is an augmented reality Pok mon game for Android and iOS mobile devices. Pok mon Go retains the basics of the original Pok mon games such as catching Pok mon, battling at Gyms, using items, evolving your creatures etc. but there is a crazy twist – you now do all this in the real world! That means instead of tapping or using a D-pad to tell your virtual avatar where to go to find Pok mon, you're actually walking. In the real world!

This game allows you to use the GPS on your smartphone to search in the real world for hidden Pok mon and capture them. With the tactile functionality included, your smartphone will vibrate to let you know when a Pok mon is nearby. To up the ante, the creators of the game allow "wild" Pok mon's – relax, this just means they only live in certain locations. So you may need to go to a lake or ocean to find water-type Pok mon, or to a local park to find grass-type Pok mon etc.

If you don't know anything about the previous games of have never played Pok mon before, that's okay! The real joy of the game is in exploring the real world with your friends, giggling while you check in at various places and making new connections in your neighborhood!

So how do I get started?

Ok, first you'll need to sing up for the game. You'll need to use your Google account or sign up for a Pok mon Trainer Club account. This is necessary because Pok mon Go stores all your information on its servers, so you'll need to use one of these two methods to link your Pok mon data to your device.

After signing up, you'll want to customize your digital avatar. You can choose your gender, eye color, hair color, shirt, hat, pants, shoes, and the style of your backpack. Once you've done so, you'll enter the main area of the game: The Pok mon Go map.

Essentially, the main area of the game is a brightly animated version of Google Maps. You'll see (unmarked) roads, rustling grass (marking Pok mon in the area), and local landmarks disguised as Pok Stops and Pok mon Gyms. As you move in the real world, your avatar does too. Pok mon will pop up on the map with a small vibration as you walk along, and if you tap on them, you can try to capture them.

- **Player icon:** Your player icon is at the bottom left corner of the screen. Tap on this to view your character's information, as well as a list of in-game achievements.
- **Backpack:** This is where all the items you pick up on your journey are stored.
- **Pok dex:** Your index of Pok mon, complete with information on all the species you've already caught.
- **Pok mon:** Here, you can see all the Pok mon that are in your possession.
- **Nearby Pok mon:** Tap on the bottom right corner of the screen to see which Pok mon are nearby.

What Pok mon Creatures Will I Encounter?

At the start, you'll only be able to catch Nintendo's original lineup of Pok mon — those found in the Red, Blue, and Yellow titles — though we expect expansions to appear as the game grows and works out the bugs.

Pok mon come in variety of types, shapes, and sizes: Of the over 100 Pok mon available for capture, you'll find creatures of the Fairy, Psychic, Electric, Grass, Water, Ghost, Bug, Rock, Ground, Poison, Flying, and Normal type. We haven't spotted any Legendary Pok mon quite yet, but that doesn't mean they aren't out there hiding.

Each geographical area has a specific Pok mon type, and some creatures are more difficult to find than others. If you keep running into the same group of Pidgey and Caterpie, don't lose hope: You need to travel around your area to find all the Pok mon. You can head to local lakes, ponds, or beaches to find Water-type Pok mon, for example, or wait until the evening to have a better chance at grabbing a Fairy type.

How do I catch my first Pok mon?

Ok, first some terminology – all Pok mon players are called "trainers" – why? Because you have to catch 'wild' Pok mon's and 'tame' them. When a trainer begins their first journey, they're given a choice of which Pok mon to start with. After you've finished customizing your avatar, three Pok mon will appear in front of you. You can choose from Bulbasaur, Charmander, or Squirtle; after capturing one, the other two will disappear.

Tip: If you walk away from the original three four times, you'll get a fourth starter Pok mon option: Pikachu.

Once you've gotten started with the game and captured your first Pok mon, it's time to go hunting for some others. You can find wild Pok mon by physically walking around your area. Pok mon appear most often near Pok Stops. The more Pok Stops nearby, the more creatures should appear.

Tip: Pok Stops are common in public places so try visiting locations with a lot of public art; tourist spots or malls are great starting points.

Isn't walking around with my eyes glued to my phone dangerous?

As you walk around in the real world, your avatar moves along the map using GPS. When a Pok mon is close enough to capture, it pops up on your screen. Since walking around with your eyes glued to your phone is a bit of a safety hazard, the game is designed to allow you to keep your eyes free while you wander. You can keep your phone at your side while you walk; when you are near a Pok mon, you'll get a notification in the form of a vibration and (if your sound is turned on) the Pok mon's unique call.

You can then move to a safe location (if you were walking along a road, for instance), and tap the visible Pok mon to capture it. Tapping zooms in on your avatar and launches an augmented reality experience with the Pok mon dancing around amidst your surroundings. If you don't see it on the screen immediately in front of you, move your device around until it appears.

Tip: There are arrows on the side of the screen to guide you in the right direction.

If Augmented Reality makes you nauseous or you don't want your battery drained, you can always turn the feature off in the upper right corner.

How do I capture a Pokémon?

Once you've found the Pokémon, it's time to throw a Pokéball to try and capture it. You "throw" in game by tapping and holding on your Pokéball; a glowing, shrinking ring appears then around the Pokémon. When the ring gets to its smallest, you want to flick your Pokéball directly toward the creature (with the aim of bopping it on the head) and release your finger; if successful, you'll capture the Pokémon inside.

Tip: Not all Pokémon enjoy being inside itty bitty areas, however, and some may jump out of your Pokéball after one or two shakes. If this happens, you'll want to throw another Pokéball to try and recapture it — or, if you're running low on supplies, run away.

As you progress in the game, you'll encounter stronger Pokémon that require a more powerful Pokéball (or Razz Berries, which lull the Pokémon to complacency). If the ring surrounding the Pokémon is green, you should have no problem capturing it; if it's yellow, you have a fifty-fifty chance; when you see a red ring, you'll need to use multiple Pokéballs, more powerful Pokéballs, or Razz Berries to have a remote chance of catching it.

More than one player can catch the same Pokémon; if you and your friend see the same Pokémon on the street, you can both grab it for your separate collections.

Tip: You can use special items to attract Pokémon to your location: You can use incense to lure Pokémon to you personally for 30 minutes, or — if you're at a Pokéstop — use a Lure Patch. This will bring Pokémon to the stop; every player there can catch them for the next 15 minutes.

What are Pokémon 'items' and how do I use them?

Items are a must-have in this game: You need Pokéballs to capture Pokémon, Incense to lure them, and potions and revives to heal them after Gym battles. Like many games of this era, you can purchase many of these items with real-world currency as transformed into Pokécoins — but you don't have to. You can stock up on most items just by visiting Pokéstops.

You never know what you're going to come across at a Pok Stop, but it's almost always helpful. Each item has a specific use in the game; most fall into either the "capture" or "recovery" category, helping you capture new Pok mon or aiding your current Pok mon in healing after Gym battles.

Tip: Incense lures Pok mon to you, Lucky Eggs grant you double experience for 30 minutes, Lure Patches, draw Pok mon to a Pok Stop, Razz Berries, make it easier to catch more of the same species of Pok mon and Pok Eggs hatch into new Pok mon.

How do I check-in at pokestops?

Look around on your map for the blue icons that denote Pokestops. These blue icons are often landmarks, sculptures, noteworthy buildings and more, and getting close to and interacting with them will score you free items like Poke Balls to catch Pok mon, Eggs to hatch Pok mon, and upon reaching level 5 - Potions and Revives to heal your Pok mon from Gym Battles. To use the Pokestop, you must move your character near enough to activate it.

Tip: there's a ring around your character that shows how close you are. Use it to your advantage! Once you have it activated, you must tap on the blue icon, then swipe to spin the blue disc that shows a picture of the spot on your screen. This will release items. You can either tap to collect them, or simply exit the Pokestop and they will be collected anyways. Note that you must remain near the Pokestop to obtain the items, which can be difficult in moving vehicles!

How easy is the game on my phone battery?

We'll level with you - Pok mon Go is quite the drain on your phone's battery. Some light searching in the tall grass of your surroundings should be fine on a half-charged phone, but for long expeditions along local routes, be sure to go out with a fully charged phone — and maybe even bring an external charger along in case things go bad while catching a Pok mon.

Tip: The app includes a "Battery Saver" option in its Settings menu, which darkens and minimizes the game when the phone is upside down (preferably in one's pocket) but still tracks and alerts when Pok mon or PokeStops are encountered. Use it!

How do I know which Pok mon is available to me?

Pok mon Go will give players an idea of the Pok mon in the nearby area with icons appearing the bottom right-hand corner of the app. They remain shrouded in shadow when you haven't yet caught that type. The mystery keeps things fun — and resembles the unknown of wandering around in the original Pok mon games — but having an idea of which Pok mon are available to you could make all the difference as you collect and train to be the very best.

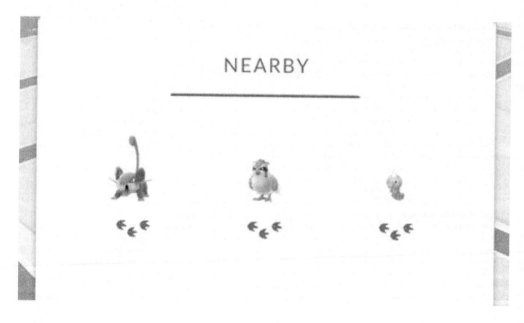

Not only will the tracker list nearby Pok mon, but also the number of footprints underneath the Pok mon will dictate how far away that Pok mon is (one footprint being close and three being farther away). You can track an individual Pok mon by tapping on it, at which point only that Pok mon will appear in the bottom right corner, and the icon will begin blink if the steps change when you are closer or further away. When the Pok mon has no footprints underneath it, will be summoned in your radius.

When you catch Pok mon, you have the option to transfer them to Professor Willow. Doing so will get you Pok mon Candy for the Pok mon you transferred, which you can then collect to eventually evolve that Pok mon, or power up their Combat Points.

Tip: before you transfer a double (or triple) to the professor, analyze the Pok mon's stats and compare it to the other Pok mon of the same kind that you already have. Which has a higher Combat Points? What attacks does each have? Which weighs more? Figure out those, and then transfer the weaker of the two.

How do I Track a Pok mon?

Tracking down, finding, and catching Pok mon in Pok mon Go requires a careful, concerted effort. Your first step is to investigate the world around you, especially rusting wild grasses you'll see on your Pok mon Go world map. Rustling wild grass does not always indicate a Pok mon. By clicking on the lower-right bar, you'll see a list of different nearby Pok mon profiles. Your phone may vibrate when nearby. You can successfully track specific Pok mon if you keep your eye on the Nearby Pok mon list. If the Pok mon icon is moving up the list to the top left spot, that means you're getting closer to it! Try going in different directions until it gets fewer footprints and moves up the list. You may find yourself right next to that elusive Scyther soon!

Tip: Pok mon will generally spawn in the same exact spot for everyone! So if you see a crowd of Trainers intensely staring at their Pok mon GO device, odds are they're catching a rare Pok mon.

Tip: sidestepping while holding the phone steady allows you to safely re-frame the Pok mon for a nice Snapshot. If AR is enabled, keep the Pok mon centered on your screen, holding your phone as still as possible. Use a gentle fingertip swipe in a straight line toward your target. You want to time your toss so that the ring around the Pok mon is contracted to its smallest when you connect. Green is best, yellow more difficult, and red a very difficult capture.

To make the capture process easier, you can switch off AR/camera mode in Pok mon Go. You can continue to walk and try to capture the Pok mon, but if you lose connection to the server in low-signal areas, you may lose the Pok mon.

How do I use Pok stops?

As we have said, Pok Stops are important or iconic places around your area: They may be special benches with dedication plaques, permanent art installations, or historic landmarks. They'll never be something as mundane as a stop sign, nor will they be in a location that is not accessible to the public — like something inside a private building, or beyond a locked gate. Pok Stops are an easy way to collect items, experience, and Pok Eggs

They're indicated on your map by tall poles with blue cube atop them: You can tap one even if you're not in range to find out which landmark they're associated with, but you won't be able to check in until you're close to the Pok Stop.

When a Pok Stop is within range, the blue cube will transform into a spinning disc, which you can tap on to visit. Inside, you'll see the Pok Stop symbol with a disc in the middle that displays the location's photo; you may also get some historical information about the monument, if you're into that sort of thing.

Tip: Swipe the disc to spin it, and you'll be rewarded with a variety of items. Items can include Pok Eggs, Pok Balls, healing potions, and more. As you increase in levels, you unlock new items to collect.

After you visit a Pok Stop, the blue pole will change to purple, and you'll be unable to visit for at least 10 minutes.

When you pick up an egg, you need to place it in an incubator to get the hatching process going. You start the game with a single, unlimited-use incubator, but you can purchase more if you want to hatch several eggs at once.

Once the egg is incubated, you'll need to physically walk — sorry, would-be cheats, but driving won't work — a certain distance before the egg will hatch. Depending on the rarity of the Pok Egg you've found, that could be as little as 2 kilometers, or up to 10 kilometers. And yes, you will have to walk with the app open for those steps to register. RIP battery life.

What Pok mon Go Doesn't tell you.

Pok mon Go can be daunting for both players new to the Pok mon franchise, and even veteran players unfamiliar with the differences from the normal Pok mon gameplay.

1. If you happen to live, work, or just be in an area near one of the Poke Stops, you'll notice that the color changes from blue to purple once interacted with. If you hang around the area for a bit, you'll find it goes back to its blue color after 5 or so minutes (times can vary), allowing you to easily stock up on poke balls and gain 50 xp, which is useful if you find yourself stuck someplace where Pok mon are not appearing.

2. Whether you're on a bus, in a car, taking a train, or whatever — you'll find that you can still play Pok mon Go on the go and your avatar will faithfully run down the streets to keep up. This can be both a blessing and a curse, because you'll often pass through several potential PokeStops or Pok mon.

   It's important to note that when interacting with PokeStops, if you leave the area, you won't be able to finish interacting with it — and interaction is often best saved when you're slowing down or stopped in a moving vehicle. However, any Pok mon that is encountered and engaged will stay with you, letting you catch them at your leisure (so long as they don't flee).

   And of course: please don't play Pok mon and drive

3. As exciting as exploring new and unknown places for Pokémon are, you won't have to brave the most dangerous places on Earth to find rare Pokémon - instead your personal level will dictate the rarity of Pokémon that appear. To start, you'll often encounter basic Pokémon (Zubats, Charmanders, Weedles, etc.) but as you gain in level, there will be a better chance of finding both Pokémon with higher Combat Power (CP), and rare Pokémon in general.

Tougher and rarer Pokémon will often be harder to catch - a green ring means an easy catch, yellow harder, and then orange and red. Difficult Pokémon may often break out of a Pokeball, or even run away. Consider using Items to make it easier before trying against these Pokémon.

4. When trying to incubate a Pokémon Egg, you'll have to travel a distance of several kilometers (varying from 2 to 5 to 10). While you might be tempted to simply drive the distance, there's more to it than distance traveled. Pokémon Go uses both your phone's pedometer as well as the GPS to calculate how far you've actually walked, and appears to limit your distance traveled if it clocks you going at high speeds. Distance traveled is still counted fairly accurately if done on a skateboard, as long as you don't go too fast.

Note: The app must be active to count your steps. This means if you go for a walk, the app must stay running and you must be logged in and playing for it to count your steps.

5. Once your trainer is level 5, you can finally visit Pok mon Gyms and battle against other trainers. If you visit a Gym with your team's color - or take over one of the opposing color, you can store your Pok mon there and become a Gym Defender. Immediately thereafter you can check the shop tab and click on the shield icon to access your Defender Bonus for free pokecoins and Stardust. Check back every 20~ hours (so long as your Pok mon have not been dethroned) and to receive more (the amount may vary depending on how many Pok mon you have in the gym, or their CP).

6. Contrary to most Pok mon games, Gym Battles in Pok mon Go are not turn based - though attacks can't be literally spammed either. To attack, simply tap the screen, and your Pok mon will deal its first attack as soon as it's able. To deal a special attack, you will need to hold down on the screen and release. In order to perform a special attack, you will need to charge the meter below a Pok mon's health until a bar is full - different special attacks have different meters.

Tip: To dodge, swipe to the sides before the attack hits.

How do I level up and evolve my Pok mon?

Evolution doesn't work the same way in Pok mon Go as it does in the classic games: Pok mon don't evolve or level up after battles with other Pok mon trainers.

Instead, you must catch duplicates of the same Pok mon, which drop Candy and Stardust. You can also send unwanted Pok mon to the Professor for a single candy, but be careful. Once a Pok mon is sent to the Professor, you can never get that version back.

Once you have gathered enough of a single type of Pok mon, you'll be able to use the Candies to evolve it. Candy is Pok mon-specific, and can be used to level up any Pok mon in that evolutionary chain. For example, you can use Candy that Charmander has dropped to evolve a Chameleon.

In addition to giving you the next evolutionary stage of a Pok mon, evolving will raise a Pok mon's CP and HP. CP represents how strong a Pok mon's attacks are while HP represents how much damage a Pok mon can take. Combining Candy and Stardust may also increase stats.

How do I join a Gym team and battle other players?

When you reach level five and visit a Gym, you'll be asked to join one of three color-coded teams: Instinct (Yellow), Mystic (Blue), or Valor (Red). They're color-coded based on the original U.S. titles – Pok mon Red, Pok mon Blue, and Pok mon Yellow: Special Pikachu Edition.
Unlike Nintendo's games, the team you choose doesn't affect the type of Pok mon you come across in the wild, but it does matter for Gym battles. After picking a team, you'll join millions of other players around the world; each team will work together to become the most successful. As with Niantic's previous title, Ingress, teams can turn Pok mon Go from a single-player experience to a group sport.
Teams are how you join up with your friends to make a dent on the world. You and your team will take over and level up Gyms; when you possess a gym, you get Pok coins and Stardust, which can help you level up and evolve your Pok mon.

Much like Pok Stops, Gyms are actual landmarks out in the world, and they are where all Pok mon battles happen. You can claim them for your team, or help level up a Gym already claimed for your team to build up its prestige. Trainers can take over an unoccupied Gym and claim it for the Instinct, Mystic, or Valor team. If your team's color is in control of a Gym, you can train your Pok mon inside, one at a time. If an opposing team holds a Gym, you'll need to battle the Pok mon standing guard to lower its prestige and have a chance of taking it over.

Gyms earn prestige when you train your Pok mon in one that your team controls, and lose prestige when opposing teams win battles against the Pok mon left there. Your team's Gym will earn experience points to gain prestige, which will amount to leveling up the Gym. As its levels increase, so do the number of Gym Leaders. For example, if your Gym has reached level three, you can have three Gym Leaders in it, which makes it harder for opposing teams to overthrow.

Entering a Gym triggers a fun mini-game wherein you attack the opposing Pok mon, and dodge their attacks. While battling, you have three options: You can tap the screen to attack, press and hold the screen to initiate a special attack, or swipe left or right to dodge an opponent's attack. Just as with traditional Pok mon games, the goal is to reduce your opponent's Pok mon to zero hit points.

Tip: To steal control of a Gym that is already occupied by an opposing team, you must win in battle against all of the Gym Leaders' Pok mon in it. Beating leaders in the Gym will lower its prestige, but it will take multiple battles against the same Pok mon in order to occupy it for your team.

When you occupy a gym, you not only help your team — but you earn Pok Coins, too! Every 20 hours, you can visit the Shop and redeem your coins, based on how many gyms you currently occupy.

How do I level up as a trainer?

Pok mon Go isn't just about taking care of and leveling your Pok mon — it's about your experience, too. You can gain levels as a trainer by catching Pok mon, exploring Pok Stops, and battling at Gyms.

As you hit higher levels, you'll be able to fight at gyms, gain access to higher-quality Pok Balls and other items, and help strengthen your Pok mon.

If you have a higher trainer level than the players at a rival Gym, you've got a better chance of taking it over. This is especially true when it comes to fighting multiple trainers to take over a single Gym.

Do you need the Pok mon Go Plus wearable?

If you decide to go all-in and invest in the $30 Pok mon Go Plus wearable, you can play the game without having to take your phone out of your pocket. The device comes with a detachable band and a clip, so you can wear it on your wrist or lapel, or backpack, or wherever.

When worn, the Pok mon Go Plus acts as a notification device, alerting you when a Pok Stop or Pok mon is nearby. You will receive a different vibration, depending on what you are near. You can then use the Pok mon Go Plus to activate a Pok Stop or even catch a Pok mon without having to look at your phone at all. To activate a Pok Stop or catch a Pok mon, you will press the wearable device in a specific pattern.

But do you need the wearable to enjoy the game? Not particularly. Your device still needs to be running Pok mon Go in the foreground, so you're not saving much battery life, and you'll get those vibrations from your iPhone or Android device, anyway.

Troubleshooting Pok mon Go

Running into crashes, problems with battery life, or glitches? We've collected some of the most common Pok mon Go problems (and their solutions) in our troubleshooting guide.

In grand Pokémon tradition, Niantic's new augmented-reality game has a few glitches, crashes, and bugs scattered in-between Pokémon Gyms, Pokéstops, and the creatures themselves.

These glitches run the gamut from momentary pauses in gameplay to getting stuck in a gym with your opponent at 1HP, and they take away from what is otherwise a delightfully fun game. It's somewhat to be expected, given the massive amount of people currently interacting with Niantic's Pokémon Go servers right about now, but that doesn't make it any less frustrating.
Unfortunately, there's no magic button you can press inside the game to instantly get it working again, but we still have some a few tips for when you run into a bug or crash while playing Pokémon Go. Here's how to get out of crash mode as quickly as possible and return to catching 'em all.

How to fix Pok mon Go crashes

Not sure whether your game has frozen or your Internet connection's just being terrible? Look for the spinning white Pokéball in the upper left corner — the game uses the icon to signify to the player that Niantic's servers are being refreshed.

If your graphics freeze but that Pokéball icon is spinning, chances are the game is just trying to connect back to its central server, and everything should catch up within a few moments. (You can also check your iPhone's status bar at the top of the screen to see the strength of your Internet connection.)

If instead, your animations resume but your buttons don't do anything and the Pokéball continues spinning, your game may have lost connection to the server and needs a reboot.

I've seen this happen several times over my last few days playing the game, but it seems to regularly happen in gyms when you bring an opponent down to 1HP. You may also catch this glitch when first launching the game, where you'll see no Pokémon nearby — nor any in your personal collection.

Try to leave the app and come back

Sometimes a quick close and re-opening is all that you need to reconnect to Niantic's servers and get back to the game.

1. Return to the **Home screen**, if you can, by pressing the Home button.
2. Open a new app, and take a few minutes to do something else. (Or better yet: Explore the area where you've been searching for Pokémon without your eyes glued to a screen!)
3. **Double-press** the Home button to enter the multitasking screen.

4. Swipe to the Pokémon Go card.
5. **Tap** on the Pokémon Go card to reenter the app.

With luck, you'll see the Gyarados loading screen and return to gym battling and creature catching in no time.

Reboot and bug report

If your game crashes, you'll unfortunately need to reboot Pokémon Go to get back to catching creatures. You may lose immediate data, but unfortunately, it seems like the only way to fix the bugs at present is to dump everything and restart. (On the plus side, if you crash during a gym fight, any damage your Pokémon have taken will be rescinded, and you'll return to them at full health.)

Here's what to do if you run into an unfixable crash.

1. Return to the **Home screen** (if you can) by pressing the Home button.
2. **Double-press** the Home button to enter the multitasking screen.
3. Swipe to the Pokémon Go card, then swipe up on the card to force quit the app.
4. **Relaunch** Pokémon Go.
5. Visit the Pokémon Go bug report page and let Niantic know about your issue.

How to stop Pokémon Go from draining your battery

Catching Pokémon may be delightful, but all of that location-awareness can wreak havoc on your iPhone's battery. Here are a few ways to keep that from happening quite so rapidly.

Turn on the Battery Saver option

Pokémon Go actually has a battery life extender option built in to the game, under the Settings pane: It's called Battery Saver. When enabled, Battery Saver mode lowers the screen brightness and reduces the refresh rates when you point the top of your phone to the ground. The Pokémon Go logo displays while doing this; you'll still get vibration notifications about nearby Pokémon, but you won't be able to see your map or check the nearby box until you once again lift your screen.

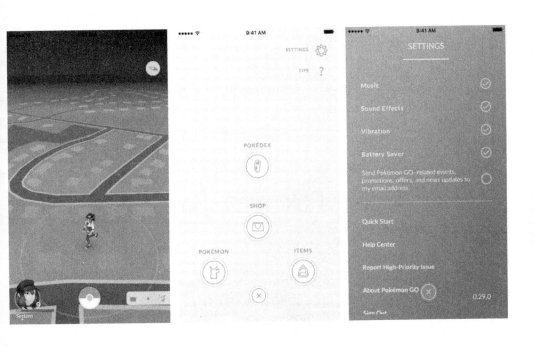

Turn off Augmented Reality

Augmented reality is a huge part of the game's appeal, to be sure: There's something delightful about seeing a Psyduck appear on your kitchen table. But AR requires turning the camera on, which puts extra strain on your battery. If you're out and about and focused on catching a bunch of creatures, you may want to focus your iPhone's longevity on that aspect, rather than on where the Pokémon were caught.

Get a battery case

It's not the best or cheapest solution, but a battery case will go a long way to keeping your battery from exploding while hunting for Pokémon or battling at gyms.

How do I play Pok mon Go when I get a server error

No one with a Pokémon addiction wants to see the fateful "Our servers are experiencing issues" message when they log in to their account over their lunch break. Unfortunately, that's what many users are getting. It's hardly a surprise: No matter how much beta-testing Niantic did before launch, millions of people want to play Pokémon Go, and most of them are awake and playing at the same time of day.

If you get an overloaded server message, chances are your server is currently capped and no more Trainers can sign in until someone else signs out. You can always wait and manually try to sign in again after a few minutes, but the quick and dirty way is to force a reboot.

1. Return to the **Home screen** (if you can) by pressing the Home button.

2. **Double-press** the Home button to enter the multitasking screen.
3. Swipe to the Pokémon Go card, then swipe up on the card to force quit the app.
4. **Relaunch** Pokémon Go and sign in.

In conclusion

We hope you have found this guide helpful! Be sure to check out our other guides and Meme books. Happy hunting!

CPSIA information can be obtained
at www.ICGtesting.com
Printed in the USA
LVOW04s1337110816

499990LV00028B/961/P